How Things Grow

From Seed
to Dandelion

By Jan Kottke

Welcome
Books

SCHOLASTIC INC.

New York   Toronto   London   Auckland   Sydney
Mexico City   New Delhi   Hong Kong

Photo Credits: Cover and all photos © Dwight Kuhn

Contributing Editors: Mark Beyer and Eliza Berkowitz
Book Design: MaryJane Wojciechowski

ISBN 0-516-23811-6

12 11 10 9 8 7 6 5 4   3 4 5 6/0

Printed in the U.S.A.

First Scholastic printing, April 2001

Contents

These are **dandelion** puff balls.

Puff balls are made of dandelion **seeds**.

5

The seeds fall off the **stem**.

The seeds are blown by the wind.

The wind carries the seeds.

They will make more dandelions.

9

A seed lands in **soil**.

A new plant is growing from the seed.

11

The dandelion flowers begin to **bloom**.

They have green leaves all around them.

Dandelions grow all over.

They grow wherever the seeds land.

15

A lot of seeds landed in this field.

Now it is covered with dandelion flowers.

17

These are full-grown dandelions.

Dandelion flowers have many **petals**.

19

Bees bring **pollen** to dandelion flowers.

Pollen helps dandelions to make seeds.

More dandelions will grow from these seeds.

21

New Words

bloom (**bloom**) to become a flower

dandelion (**dan**-dee-leyen) a flower with yellow petals

petals (**peh**-tuhlz) a part of a flower

pollen (**pah**-len) a powder that helps flowers make seeds

seeds (**seedz**) the small parts of plants that grow into new plants

soil (**soyl**) dirt

stem (**stem**) thin part of a plant that grows from the ground

To Find Out More

Books

A Dandelion's Life
by John Himmelman
Children's Press

Dandelions
by Kathleen V. Kudlinski
The Lerner Publishing Group

Dandelion
by Barry Watts
Silver Burdett Press

The Dandelion Seed
by Joseph A. Anthony
Dawn Publications

Web Sites

The Dandelion
www.cyberfair.org/ntrail/ntweb1/ndandeli.html
Learn more about dandelions, including what they look like and when they grow.

What is a Flower?
http://tqjunior.advanced.org/3715/flower.html
This site tells the story of flowers and how plants grow.

Index

About the Author

Jan Kottke is the owner/director of several preschools in the Tidewater area of Virginia. A lifelong early education professional, she is completing a phonics reading series for preschoolers.

Reading Consultants

Kris Flynn, Coordinator, Small School District Literacy, The San Diego County Office of Education

Shelly Forys, Certified Reading Recovery Specialist, W.J. Zahnow Elementary School, Waterloo, IL

Peggy McNamara, Professor, Bank Street College of Education, Reading and Literacy Program

Early
Interven
Level
13

WELCOME
to Reading!

WELCOME BOOKS

provide children with a fun and exciting introduction to reading
about the people, places, and things in their world.

This edition is on
available for distribu
through the school ma

SCHOLASTIC IN

0-516-23811-6